HAL LEONARD — CHRISTMAS PIANO FOR TEENS

PIANO METHOD

T0039486

12 Popular Christmas Solos for Beginners

ARRANGED BY JENNIFER LINN

Speed • Pitch • Balance • Loop

To access audio visit:
www.halleonard.com/mylibrary

Enter Code
6224-2082-5831-5232

ISBN: 978-1-5400-3121-1

Visit Hal Leonard Online at
www.halleonard.com

Contact Us:
Hal Leonard
7777 West Bluemound Road
Milwaukee, WI 53213
Email: info@halleonard.com

In Europe contact:
Hal Leonard Europe Limited
42 Wigmore Street
Marylebone, London, W1U 2RN
Email: info@halleonardeurope.com

In Australia contact:
Hal Leonard Australia Pty. Ltd.
4 Lentara Court
Cheltenham, Victoria, 3192 Australia
Email: info@halleonard.com.au

INTRODUCTION

Christmas Piano For Teens is a supplementary piano solo book for beginners and written to coordinate perfectly with the *Piano For Teens Method Book*. Like the method book, the songs begin with easy-to-read music notation with note names inside the note heads. Later in the book, the songs progress to adding simple left-hand chord accompaniments to favorite holiday tunes. The book includes access to audio tracks online for download or streaming, using the unique code inside this book!

–Jennifer Linn

ABOUT THE AUDIO

To access the accompanying audio, simply go to **www.halleonard.com/mylibrary** and enter the code found on page 1 of this book. This will grant you instant access to every file. You can download to your computer, tablet, or phone, or stream the audio live—and you can also use our *PLAYBACK+* multi-functional audio player to slow down or speed up the tempo, change keys, or set loop points. This feature is available exclusively from Hal Leonard and is included with the price of this book!

For technical support, please email support@halleonard.com

CONTENTS

JOLLY OLD ST. NICHOLAS

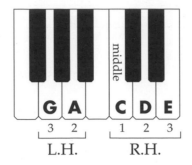

Traditional 19th Century American Carol

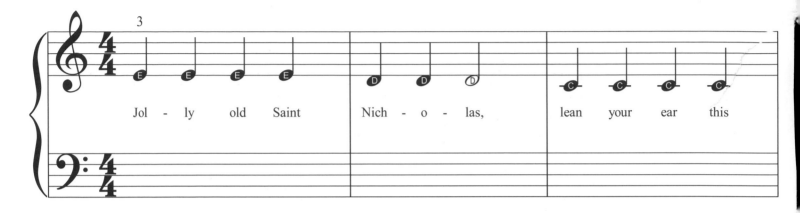

Jol - ly old Saint Nich - o - las, lean your ear this

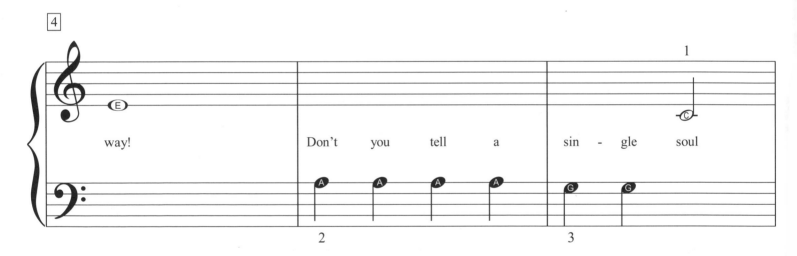

way! Don't you tell a sin - gle soul

Teacher Duet (Student plays two octaves higher than written.)

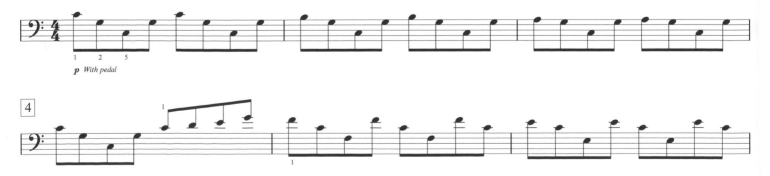

p With pedal

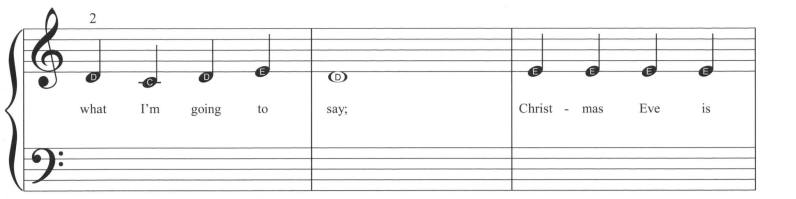

what   I'm   going   to   say;   Christ - mas   Eve   is

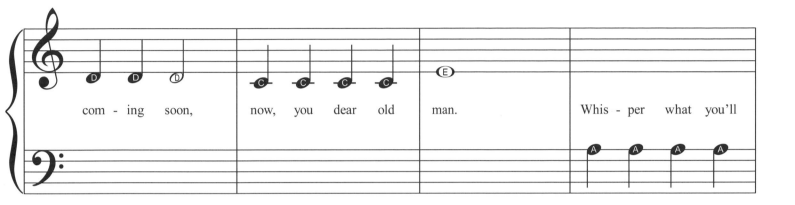

com - ing   soon,   now,   you   dear   old   man.   Whis - per   what   you'll

Play the next highest C on your piano

3

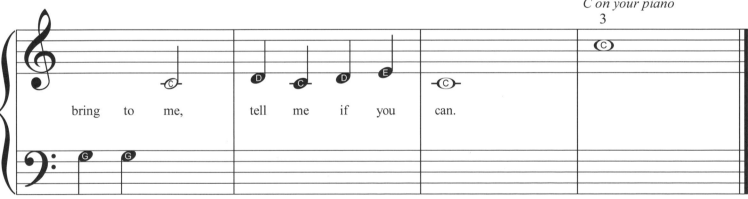

bring   to   me,   tell   me   if   you   can.

7

10

14

5

JINGLE BELLS

**Words and Music by
J. Pierpont**

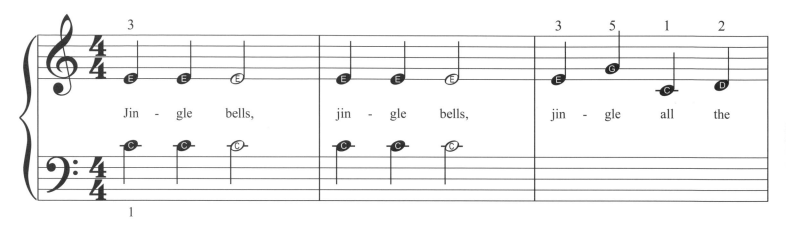

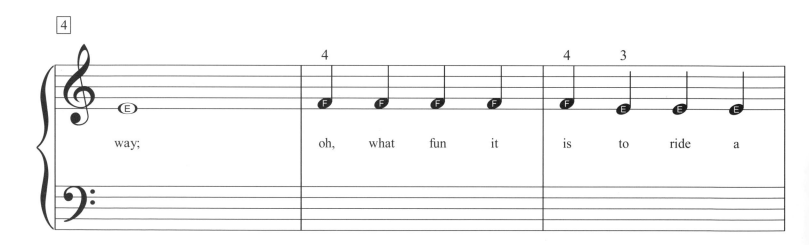

Teacher Duet (Student plays as written.)

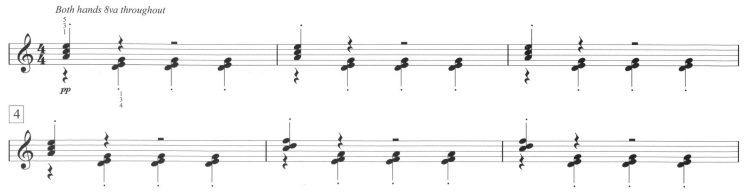

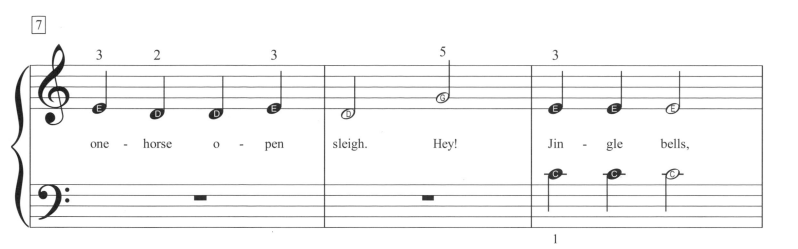

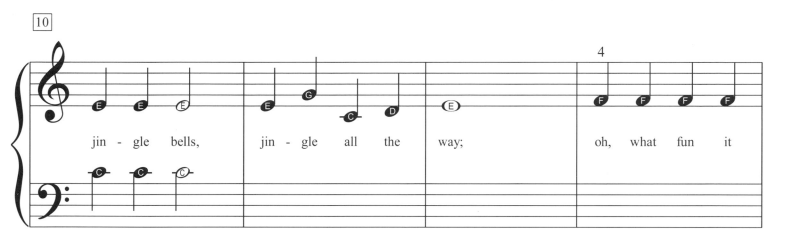

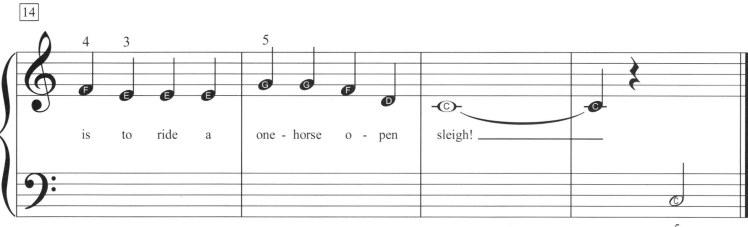

*play the next lowest
C on your piano*

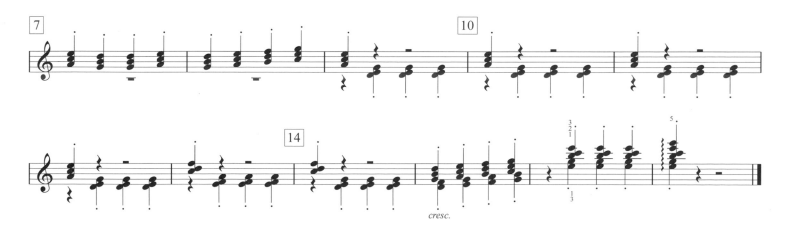

THE LITTLE DRUMMER BOY

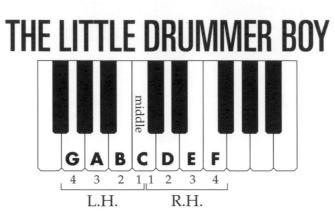

Words and Music by Harry Simeone,
Henry Onorati and Katherine Davis

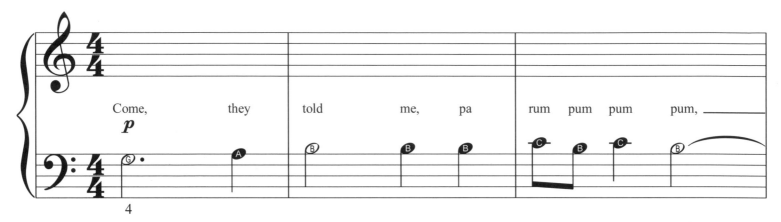

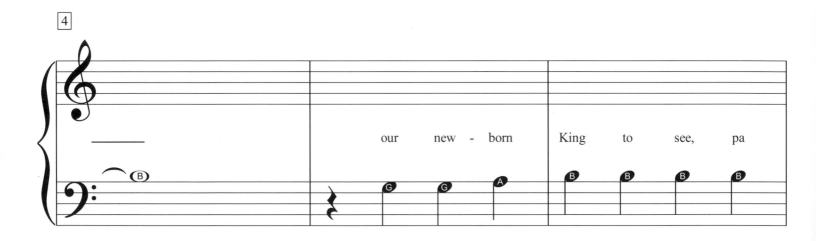

Teacher Duet (Student plays one octave higher than written.)

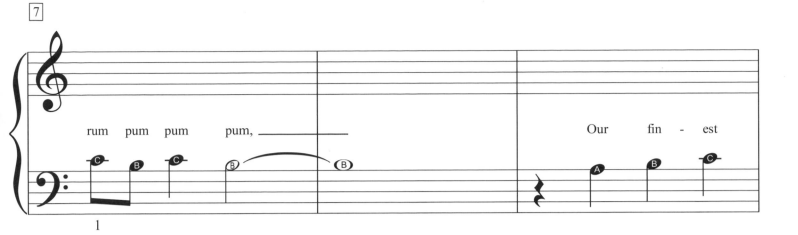

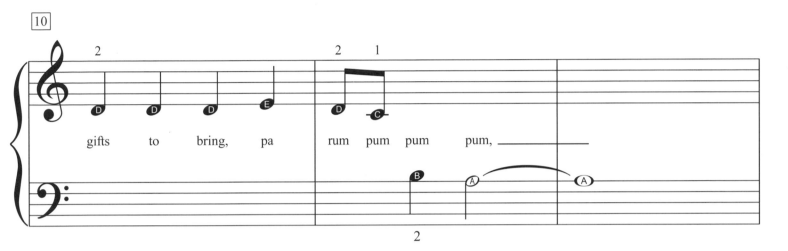

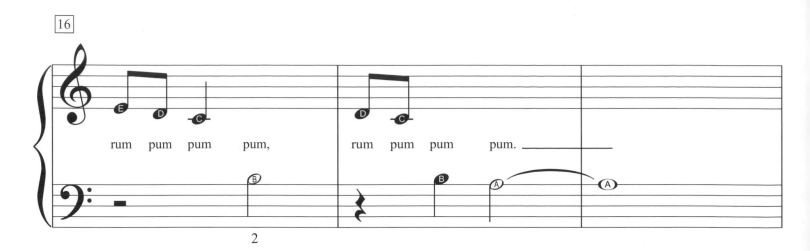

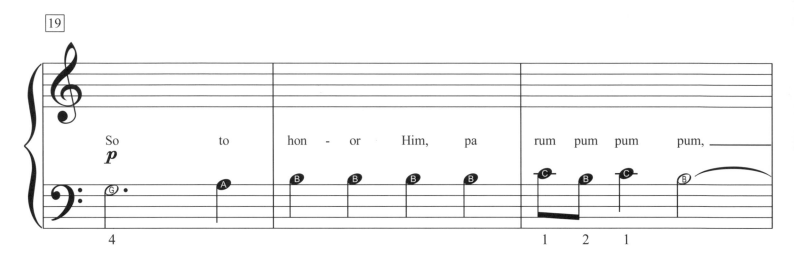

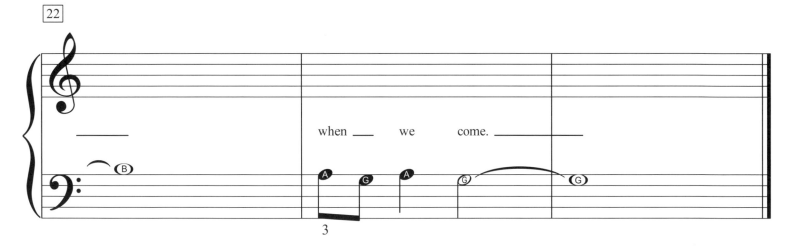

MARY, DID YOU KNOW?

HAND POSITION SHIFT

In this book, when you see a fingering in a shaded triangle, your hand will need to move higher or lower on the keyboard depending on the direction of the triangle.

Words and Music by Mark Lowry and Buddy Greene

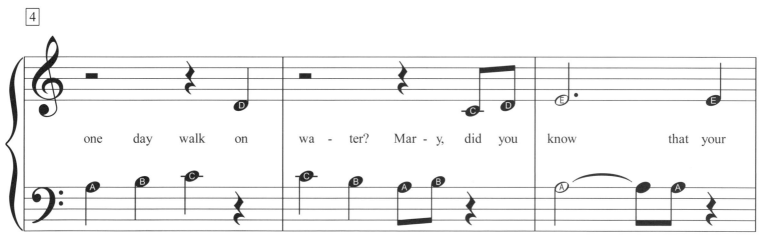

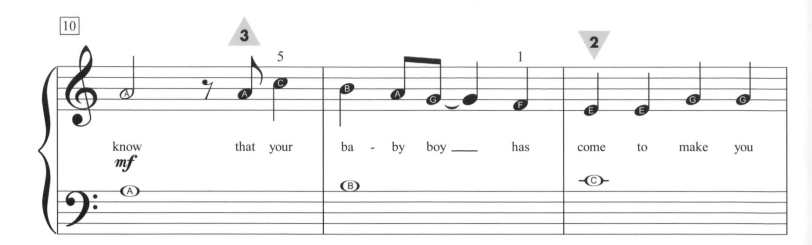

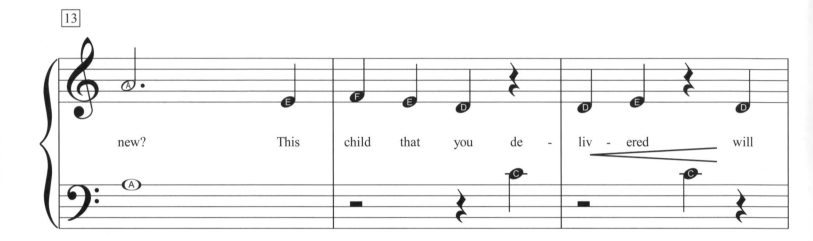

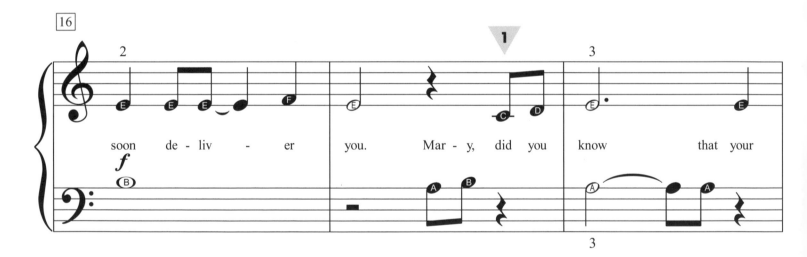

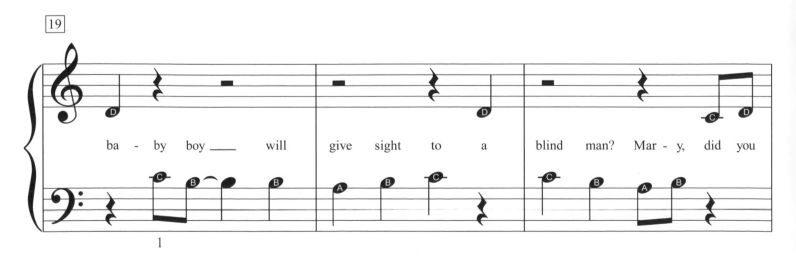

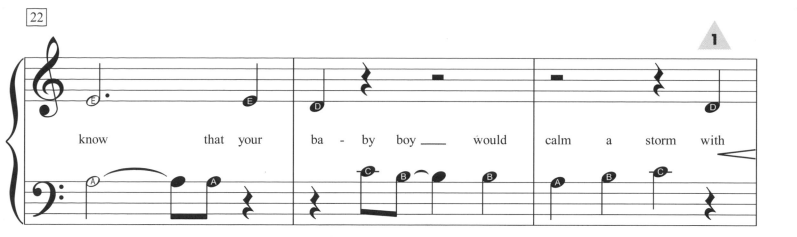

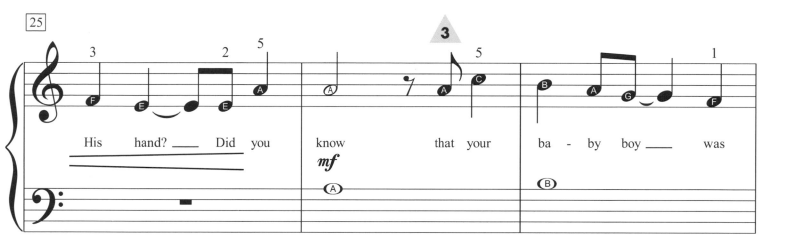

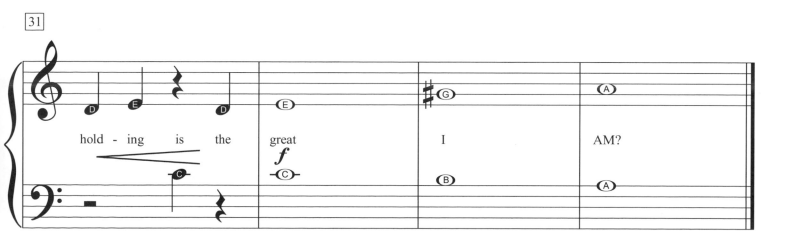

SLEIGH RIDE

Music by Leroy Anderson

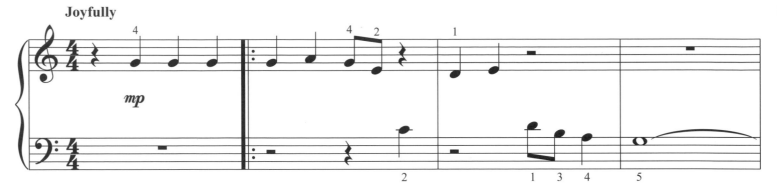

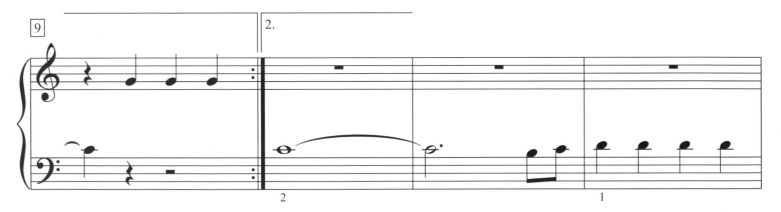

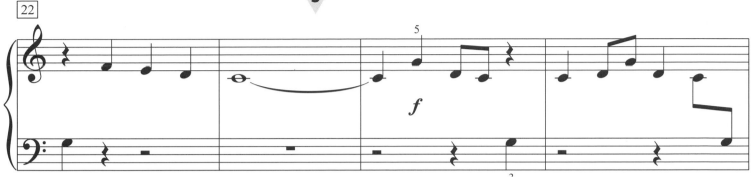

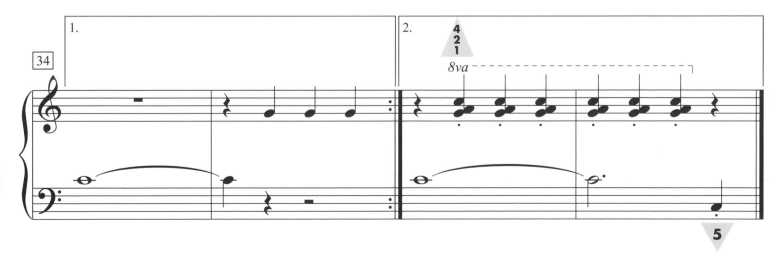

JINGLE BELL ROCK

Words and Music by Joe Beal
and Jim Boothe

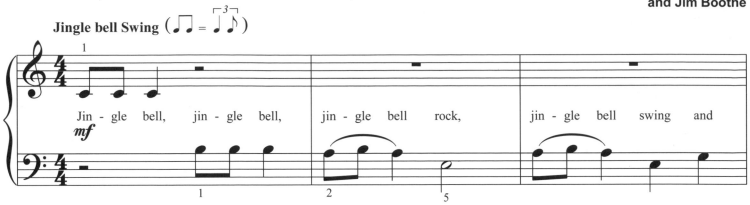

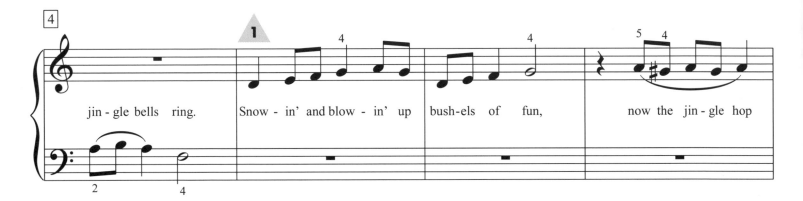

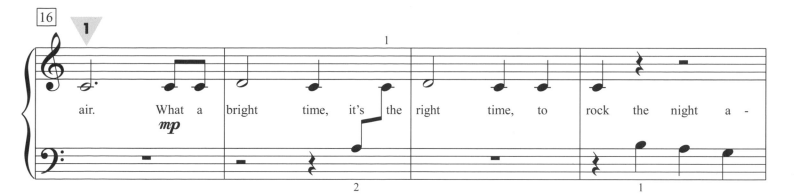

air. What a bright time, it's the right time, to rock the night a-

way. Jin - gle bell time is a swell time to go glid - in' in a

one - horse sleigh. Gid - dy - ap, jin - gle horse, pick up your feet,

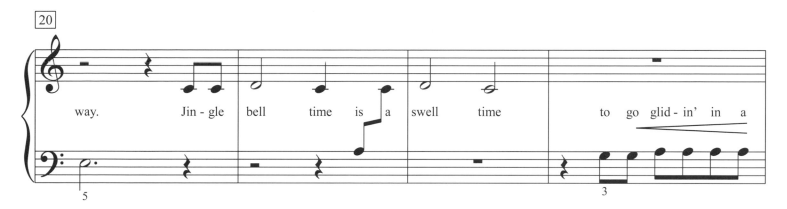

jin - gle a - round the clock. Mix and min - gle in a jin - gl - in' beat,

that's the jin - gle bell, that's the jin - gle bell, that's the jin - gle bell rock.

17

SANTA BABY

By Joan Javits,
Phil Springer and Tony Springer

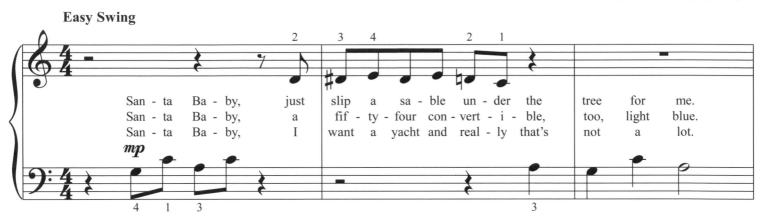

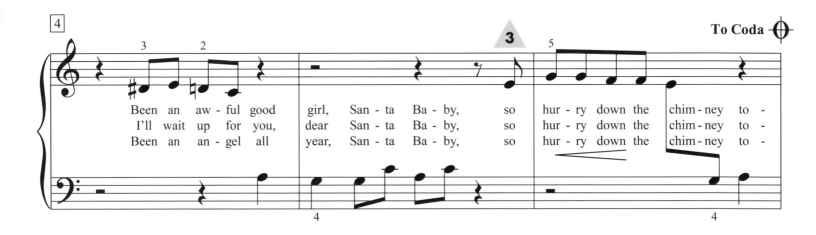

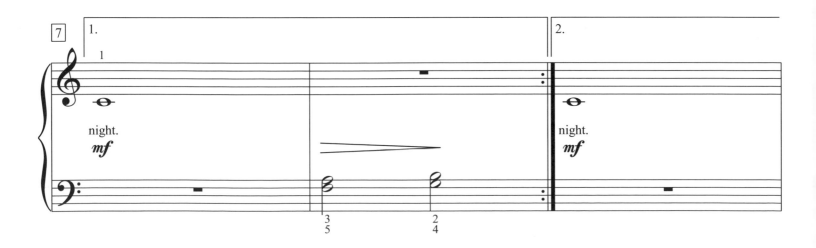

Think of all the fun I've missed

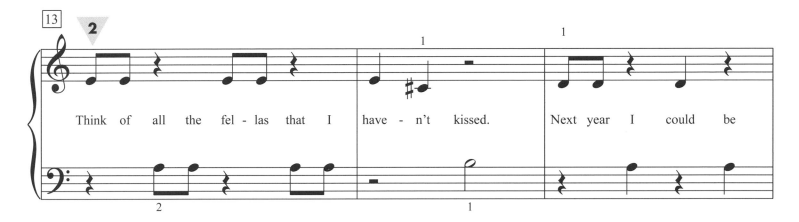

Think of all the fel-las that I have-n't kissed. Next year I could be

D.C. al Coda
(Go to the beginning, and
then at the ⊕ sign, jump to the
Coda at the end of the song.)

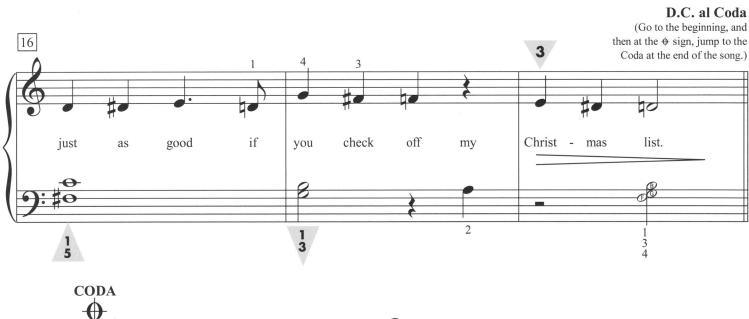

just as good if you check off my Christ-mas list.

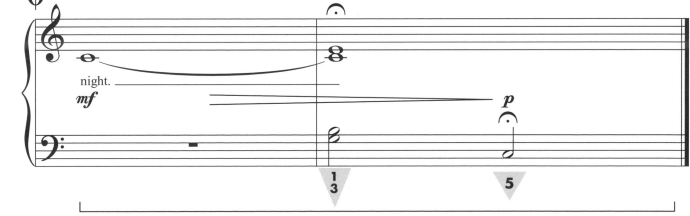

CODA

night.

mf

p

CHORD WARM-UPS

- Practice these L.H. chord warm-ups slowly and use the exact fingering as shown. Keep a rounded hand shape and play with slightly curved fingers. Use your arm weight to synchronize playing 3 keys at once.

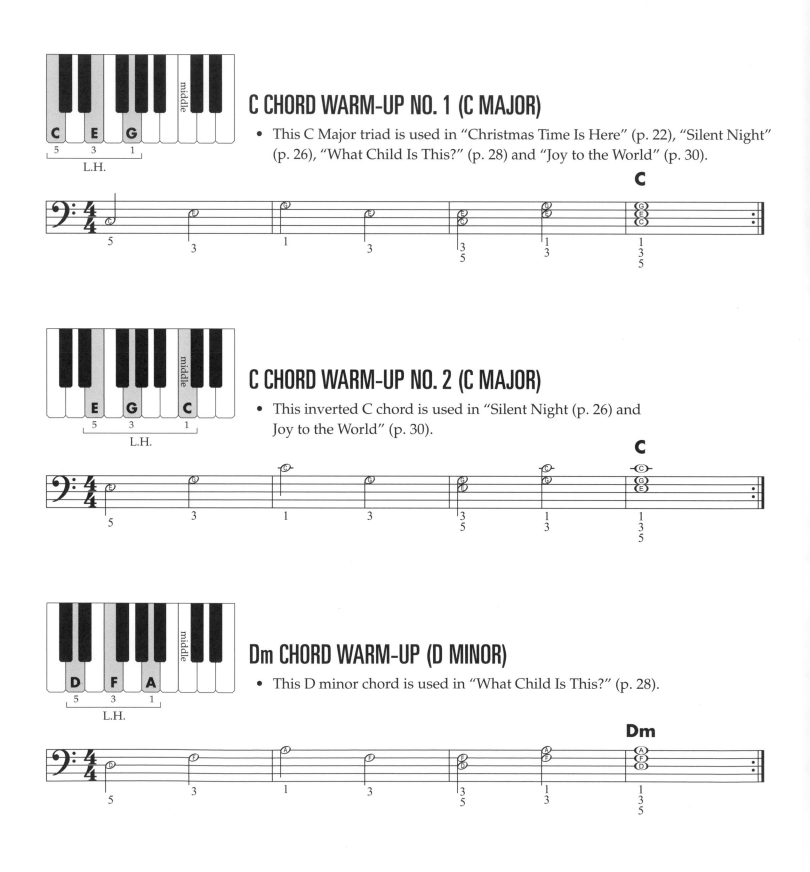

C CHORD WARM-UP NO. 1 (C MAJOR)

- This C Major triad is used in "Christmas Time Is Here" (p. 22), "Silent Night" (p. 26), "What Child Is This?" (p. 28) and "Joy to the World" (p. 30).

C CHORD WARM-UP NO. 2 (C MAJOR)

- This inverted C chord is used in "Silent Night (p. 26) and Joy to the World" (p. 30).

Dm CHORD WARM-UP (D MINOR)

- This D minor chord is used in "What Child Is This?" (p. 28).

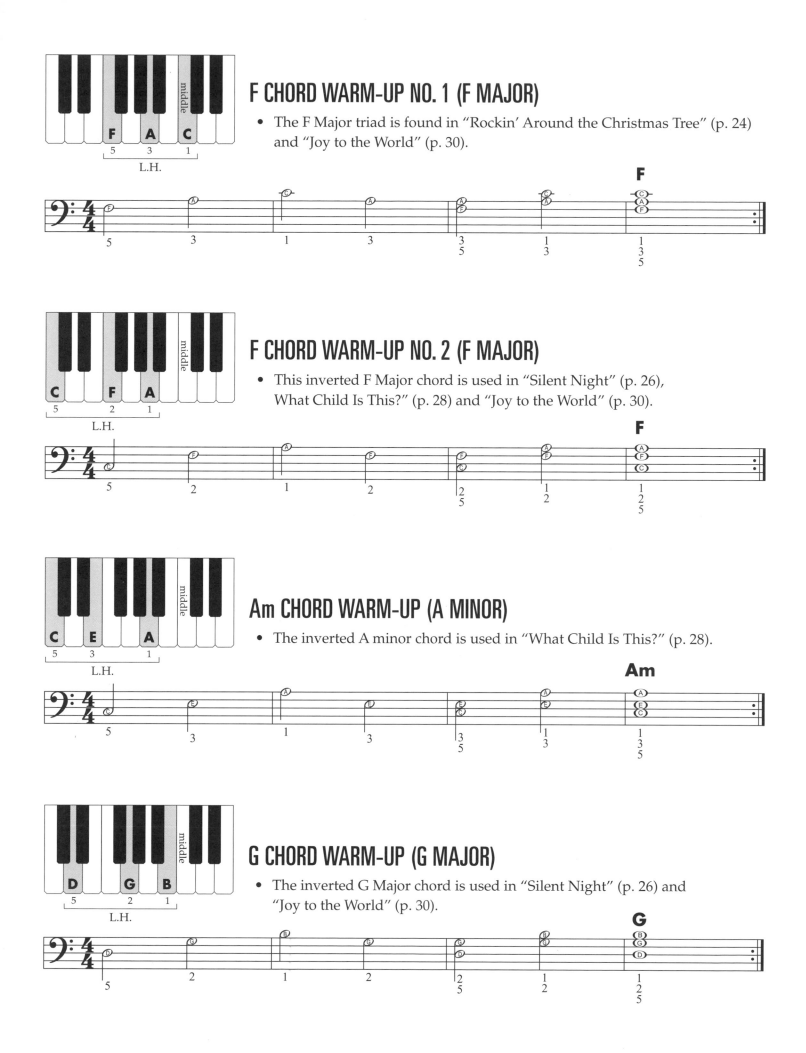

F CHORD WARM-UP NO. 1 (F MAJOR)

- The F Major triad is found in "Rockin' Around the Christmas Tree" (p. 24) and "Joy to the World" (p. 30).

F CHORD WARM-UP NO. 2 (F MAJOR)

- This inverted F Major chord is used in "Silent Night" (p. 26), What Child Is This?" (p. 28) and "Joy to the World" (p. 30).

Am CHORD WARM-UP (A MINOR)

- The inverted A minor chord is used in "What Child Is This?" (p. 28).

G CHORD WARM-UP (G MAJOR)

- The inverted G Major chord is used in "Silent Night" (p. 26) and "Joy to the World" (p. 30).

CHRISTMAS TIME IS HERE
from A CHARLIE BROWN CHRISTMAS

Words by Lee Mendelson
Music by Vince Guaraldi

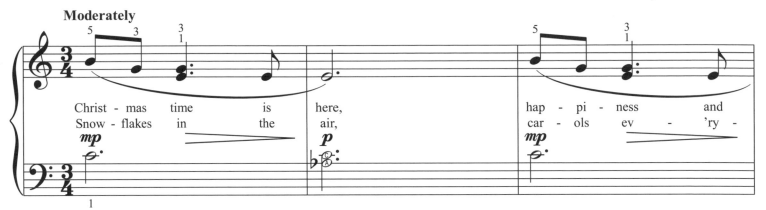

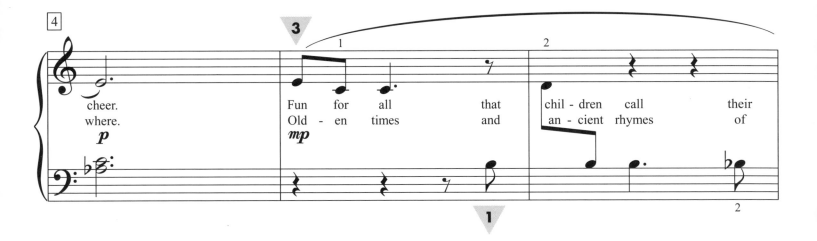

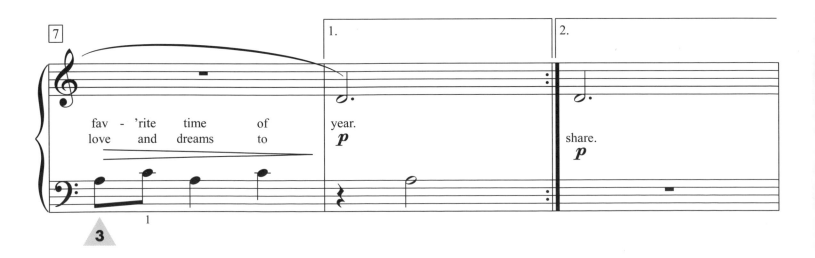

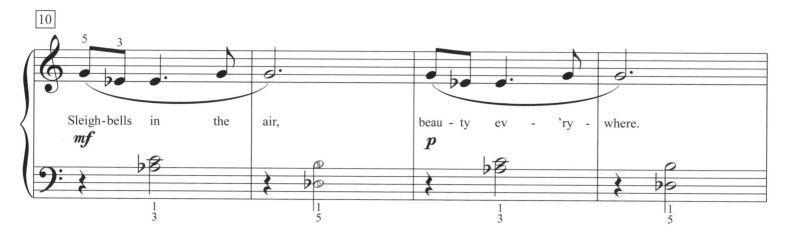

ROCKIN' AROUND THE CHRISTMAS TREE

Music and Lyrics by
Johnny Marks

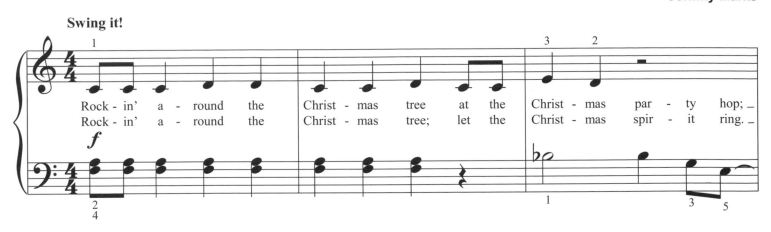

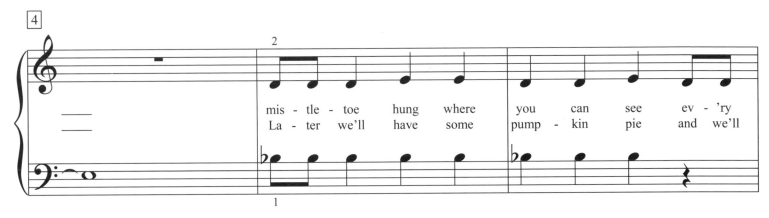

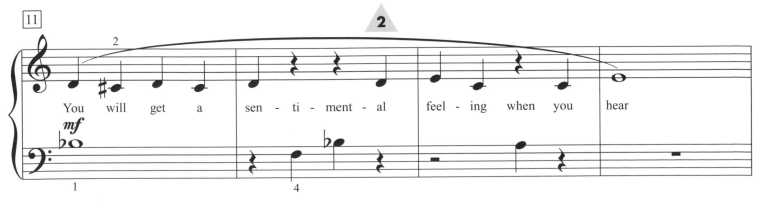

voic - es sing - ing, "Let's be jol - ly, deck the halls with boughs of hol - ly."

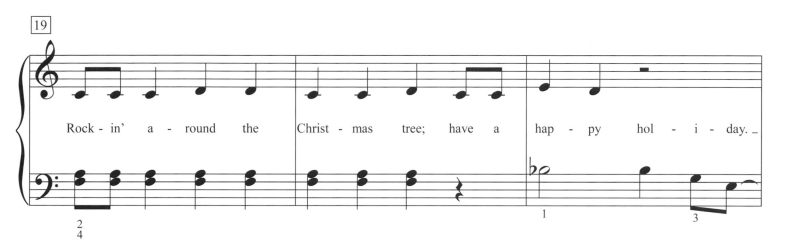

Rock - in' a - round the Christ - mas tree; have a hap - py hol - i - day.

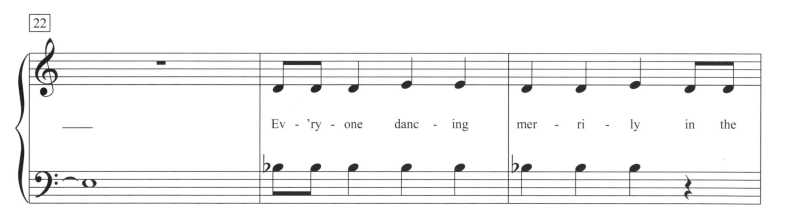

Ev - 'ry - one danc - ing mer - ri - ly in the

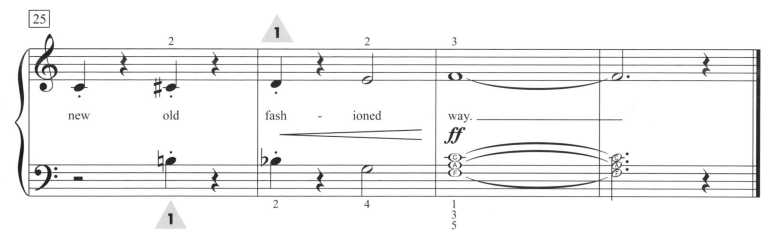

new old fash - ioned way.

SILENT NIGHT

Words by Joseph Mohr
Translated by John F. Young
Music by Franz X. Gruber

Peacefully

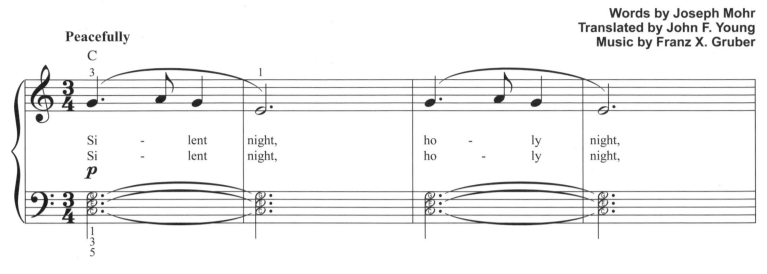

Si - lent night, ho - ly night,
Si - lent night, ho - ly night,

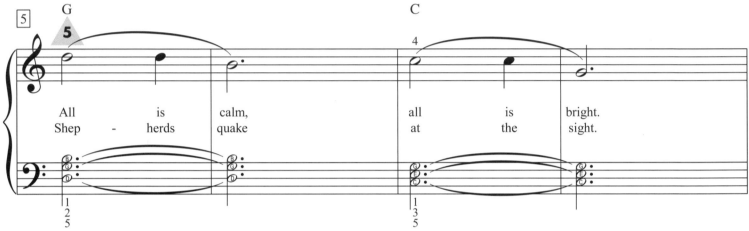

All is calm, all is bright.
Shep - herds quake at the sight.

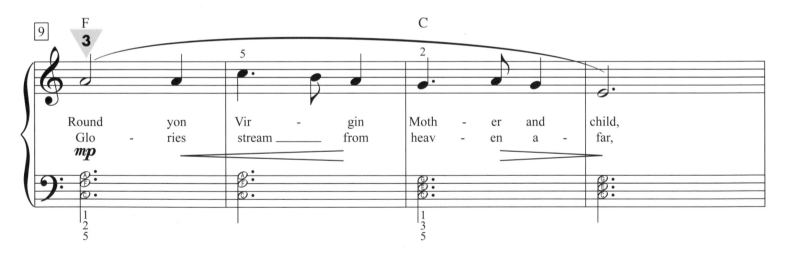

Round yon Vir - gin Moth - er and child,
Glo - ries stream from heav - en a - far,

Teacher Duet (Student plays as written.)

ho - ly in - fant so ten - der and mild,
heaven - ly hosts _____ sing Al - le - lu - ia.

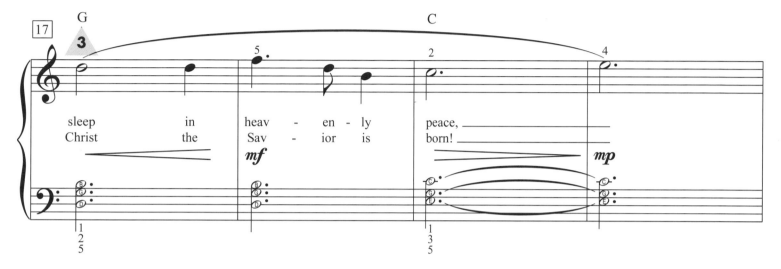

sleep in heav - en - ly peace, _____
Christ in the Sav - ior is born! _____

mf

mp

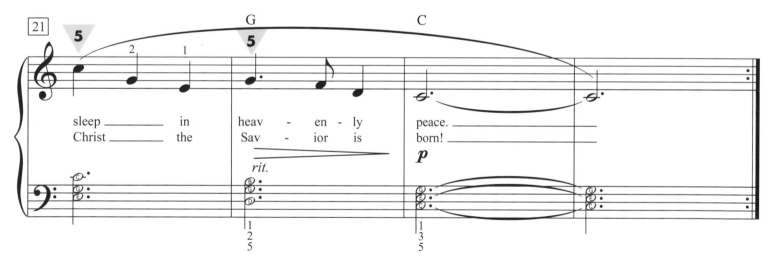

sleep _____ in heav - en - ly peace. _____
Christ _____ the Sav - ior is born! _____

rit.

p

rit.

WHAT CHILD IS THIS?

Words by William C. Dix
16th Century English Melody

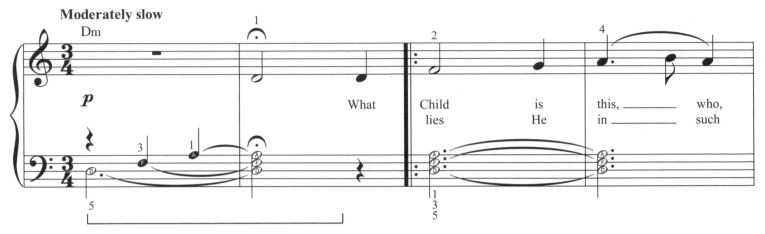

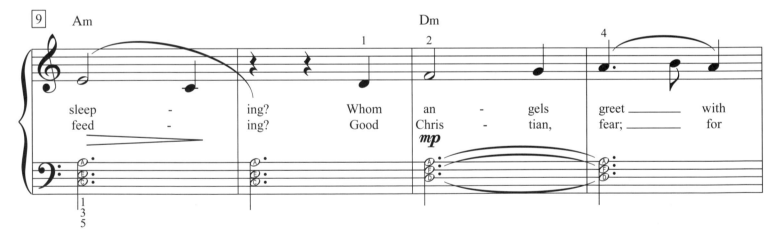

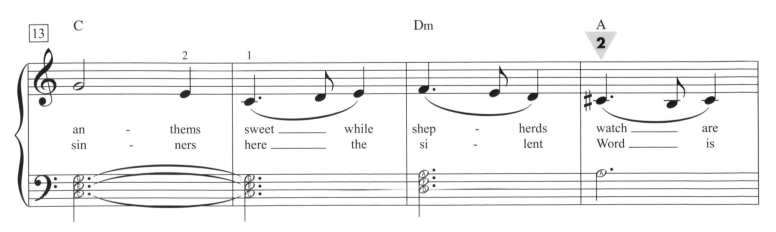

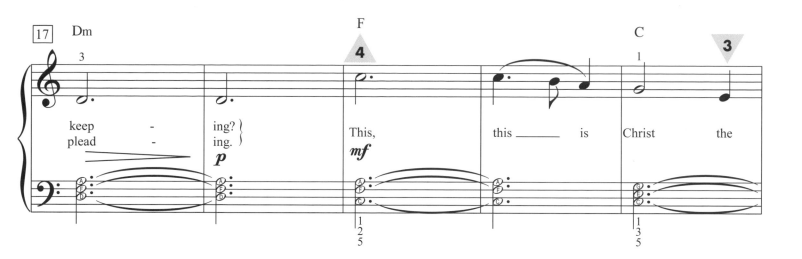

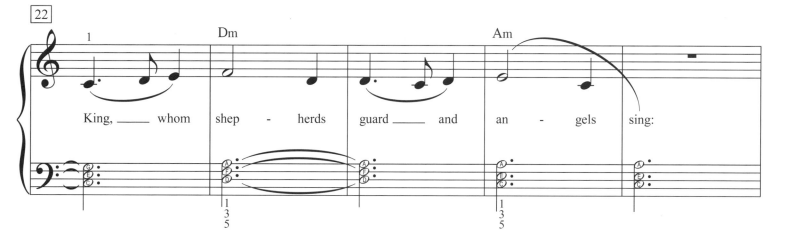

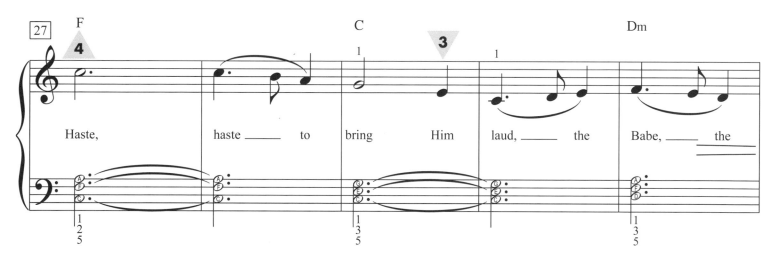

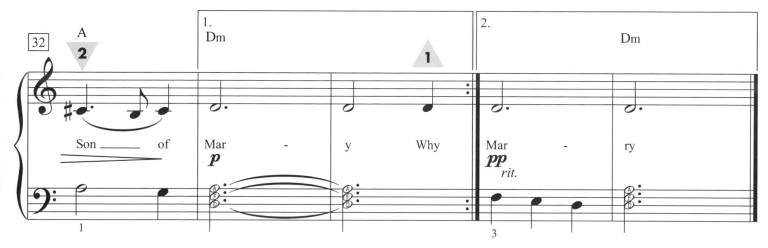

JOY TO THE WORLD

Words by Isaac Watts
Music by George Frideric Handel
Adapted by Lowell Mason

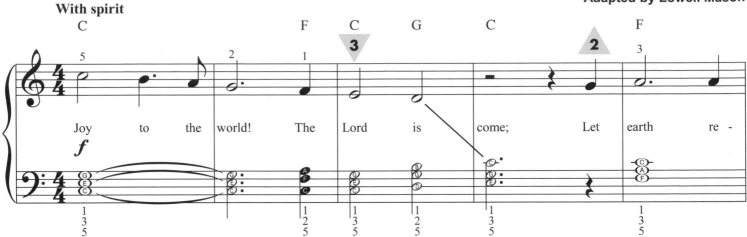

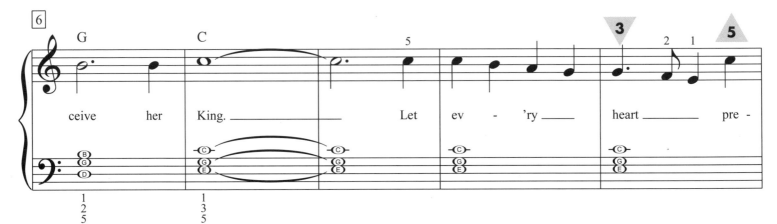

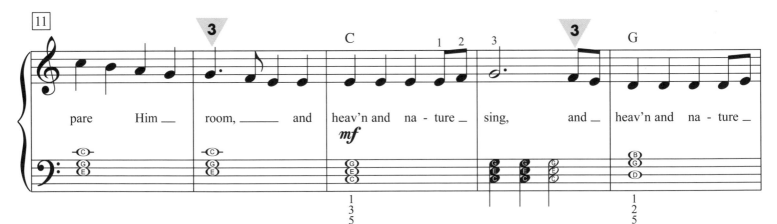

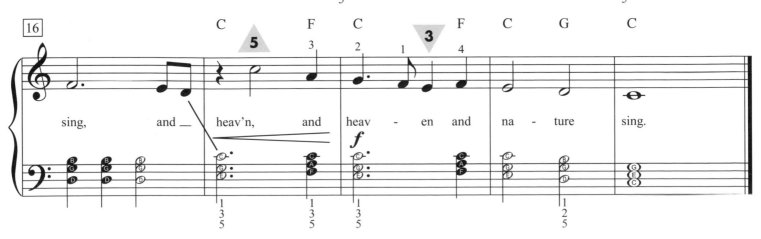

PoP PIANO HITS

Pop Piano Hits is a series designed for students of all ages. Each book contains five simple and easy-to-read arrangements of today's most popular downloads. Lyrics, fingering and chord symbols are included to help you make the most of each arrangement. Enjoy your favorite songs and artists today!

BELIEVER, WHAT ABOUT US & MORE HOT SINGLES

Attention (Charlie Puth) • Believer (Imagine Dragons) • There's Nothing Holdin' Me Back (Shawn Mendes) • Too Good at Goodbyes (Sam Smith) • What About Us (P!nk).

00251934 Easy Piano $9.99

BLANK SPACE, I REALLY LIKE YOU & MORE HOT SINGLES

Blank Space (Taylor Swift) • Heartbeat Song (Kelly Clarkson) • I Really Like You (Carly Rae Jepsen) • I'm Not the Only One (Sam Smith) • Thinking Out Loud (Ed Sheeran).

00146286 Easy Piano $9.99

CAN'T STOP THE FEELING, 7 YEARS & MORE HOT SINGLES

Can't Stop the Feeling (Justin Timberlake) • H.O.L.Y. (Florida Georgia Line) • Just Like Fire (Pink) • Lost Boy (Ruth B.) • 7 Years (Lukas Graham).

00193755 Easy Piano $9.99

CITY OF STARS, MERCY & MORE HOT SINGLES

City of Stars (from *La La Land*) • Evermore (from *Beauty and the Beast*) • Mercy (Shawn Mendes) • Perfect (Ed Sheeran) • Stay (Zedd & Alessia Cara).

00236097 Easy Piano $9.99

FEEL IT STILL, REWRITE THE STARS & MORE HOT SINGLES

Feel It Still (Portugal. The Man) • Lost in Japan (Shawn Mendes) • The Middle (Zedd, Maren Morris & Grey) • Rewrite the Stars (from *The Greatest Showman*) • Whatever It Takes (Imagine Dragons).

00278090 Easy Piano $9.99

GIRLS LIKE YOU, HAPPY NOW & MORE HOT SINGLES

Girls Like You (Maroon 5) • Happy Now (Zedd feat. Elley Duhé) • Treat Myself (Meghan Trainor) • You Are the Reason (Calum Scott) • You Say (Lauren Daigle).

00285014 Easy Piano $9.99

HELLO, BETTER WHEN I'M DANCIN' & MORE HOT SINGLES

Better When I'm Dancin' (Meghan Trainor) • Burning House (Cam) • Drag Me Down (One Direction) • Hello (Adele) • She Used to Be Mine (Sara Bareilles).

00156235 Easy Piano $9.99

HOW FAR I'LL GO, THIS TOWN & MORE HOT SINGLES

How Far I'll Go (Alessia Cara - from *Moana*) • My Way (Calvin Harris) • This Town (Niall Horan) • Treat You Better (Shawn Mendes) • We Don't Talk Anymore (Charlie Puth feat. Selena Gomez).

00211286 Easy Piano $9.99

LET IT GO, HAPPY & MORE HOT SINGLES

All of Me (John Legend) • Dark Horse (Katy Perry) • Happy (Pharrell) • Let It Go (Demi Lovato) • Pompeii (Bastille).

00128204 Easy Piano $9.99

LOVE YOURSELF, STITCHES & MORE HOT SINGLES

Like I'm Gonna Lose You (Meghan Trainor) • Love Yourself (Justin Bieber) • One Call Away (Charlie Puth) • Stitches (Shawn Mendes) • Stressed Out (Twenty One Pilots).

00159285 Easy Piano $9.99

ROAR, ROYALS & MORE HOT SINGLES

Atlas (Coldplay – from *The Hunger Games: Catching Fire*) • Roar (Katy Perry) • Royals (Lorde) • Safe and Sound (Capital Cities) • Wake Me Up! (Avicii).

00123868 Easy Piano $9.99

SAY SOMETHING, COUNTING STARS & MORE HOT SINGLES

Counting Stars (One Republic) • Demons (Imagine Dragons) • Let Her Go (Passenger) • Say Something (A Great Big World) • Story of My Life (One Direction).

00125356 Easy Piano $9.99

SEE YOU AGAIN, FLASHLIGHT & MORE HOT SINGLES

Budapest (George Ezra) • Flashlight (Jessie J.) • Honey I'm Good (Andy Grammer) • See You Again (Wiz Khalifa) • Shut Up and Dance (Walk the Moon).

00150045 Easy Piano $9.99

SHAKE IT OFF, ALL ABOUT THAT BASS & MORE HOT SINGLES

All About That Bass (Meghan Trainor) • Shake It Off (Taylor Swift) • A Sky Full of Stars (Coldplay) • Something in the Water (Carrie Underwood) • Take Me to Church (Hozier).

00142734 Easy Piano $9.99

HAL•LEONARD®

Prices, contents and availability subject to change without notice.

www.halleonard.com

0818
186